GALLERY OF
STEAM

First published in 2004

A catalogue record for this book is available from the British Library

ISBN 1 84425 160 8

Published jointly by
Haynes Publishing, Sparkford,
Yeovil, Somerset BA22 7JJ, England
Phone 01963 440635,
www.haynes.co.uk
And
Emap Active Limited,
Wentworth House, Wentworth Street,
Peterborough PE1 1DS, England
Phone 01733 213700,
www.emap.com

Produced for Haynes Publishing and Emap Active Ltd by
PAGE One, 5 Missenden Road, Chesham, Bucks HP5 1JL, England

Printed and bound in England by J.H. Haynes & Co. Ltd, Sparkford

Contents

Until its preservation 50 years ago, the Ffestiniog Railway was most certainly a steam byway for passenger traffic. Creating an almost three-dimensional image against a rocky escarpment near Tanygrisiau, 'Single' Fairlie 0-4-4T Taliesin scuttles along its embankment on February 27 2003.
PETER SKELTON

Foreword

Welcome to 'Gallery of Steam', a collection of some of the finest photographs to have graced the pages of *Steam Railway* magazine in recent years. Steam locomotives, and the steam age railway, are intensely photographic subjects: the exhaust from a hard working engine on a crisp winter's day, the fire, the smoke, the movement of the engine itself and its interplay with the landscape around it... the steam railway can form stunning images.

Ever since its inception in 1979, *Steam Railway* has been a forum for the very best steam pictures, both the conventional and more avant garde.

Long-running features such as 'The Glorious Years' (featuring working British steam before it finished on BR in 1968) and Gallery - the best of steam today - have become institutions. That's been down purely to the dedication, skill and enthusiasm of the hundreds of photographers who contribute to the magazine. It's in large part due to them that *Steam Railway* has been the world's biggest selling steam magazine from the start.

Many photographers think nothing of driving hundreds of miles just to get one picture. Others go to extraordinary lengths to recreate scenes from 40 or more years ago. Yet others will trek around the world to hunt out the very last steam locomotives still working for their living, to capture them on film before it's too late.

This book is about the steam engines, but it's a tribute to the photographers and their pictures. Thanks to all of them - and we hope you enjoy this 'Gallery of Steam'.

Tony Streeter
EDITOR, STEAM RAILWAY

The publisher would like to acknowledge the diligent efforts of Susan Voss, Mel Holley and the staff of Emap Licensing for making this project possible.

Main line MAGIC

For many, the greatest steam thrill is to see a locomotive thundering along, working hard with a heavy train. That means that although some marvellous branch lines and secondary routes have been saved by the preservationists, there's really only one place to see the very largest locomotives doing what they were built for – on the main lines of the national railway.

More than thirty-five years after the end of British Rail steam, running these locomotives on the main line is becoming gradually ever harder, but there are still many dedicated groups who overcome all the obstacles. Whether it's in the north of Scotland, west Wales, the Midlands or the busy commuter lines out of London, there's almost nowhere that's been untouched by special steam-hauled excursions. The chances are, if you want to travel on a steam-hauled train near you, you can find one.

Long may that continue.

A very special moment on the North Wales coast as LMS 'Duchess' 4-6-2 No. 6233 *Duchess of Sutherland* races past Llanfairfechan on June 11 2002 with the Royal Train from Holyhead to Crewe, as part of HM The Queen's Golden Jubilee celebrations.
EDDIE BOBROWSKI

◄ Doing what LNER 'V2' class 2-6-2s do best – working hard – No. 60800 *Green Arrow* storms up the 1-in-187 gradient at Fosse Road near Leamington Spa, Warwickshire on September 15 2001. The 1936-built locomotive is owned by the National Railway Museum, York, who's representative, Ray Towell, is beaming from the fireman's seat in the cab.
DAVID HOLMAN

▼ With a rake of vintage coaches in tow, hauled by a 4-4-0, at first glance this might be mistaken for a preserved railway. But it is not – it's broad gauge main line steam, Northern Ireland style. The Railway Preservation Society of Ireland's 4-4-0 No. 171 *Slieve Gullion* departs from Castlerock station, heading for Londonderry on May 13 2001.
MIKE DODD

◄ The glory that is the Settle & Carlisle line, which famously runs over the 'roof of England.' LMS Stanier 'Pacific' No. 6233 *Duchess of Sutherland* roars southbound towards Ais Gill summit with 'The Midland Coronation' on July 20 2002. ANDREW RAPACZ

▼ Perfect winter conditions for LMS Stanier 'Pacific' No. 46203 *Princes Margaret Rose* as it races out of Milford Tunnel, Derbyshire, with 'The Waverley' from Leicester to Carlisle on January 2 1995. LES NIXON

It's full tide and full sun for the GWR 4-6-0 duo of Nos. 4936 *Kinlet Hall* and 5029 *Nunney Castle* as they accelerate past Starcross, Devon, with 'The Double Duchy' from Taunton to Penzance on April 7 2001.
DAVID HOLMAN

Working on the summer Fort William–Mallaig tourist train, LNER 'K1' 2-6-0 No. 62005 blasts up Beasdale bank on September 20 2001. Run by West Coast Railways, the regular train is one of the area's leading tourist attractions.
PETER VAN CAMPENHOUT

Very firmly on 'home' territory, SR Bulleid 'Pacific' No. 34016 *Bodmin* makes a rousing departure from Salisbury, whose Cathedral spire, the tallest in Britain, stands proudly in the background. This was *Bodmin's* first public main line run, 'The Phoenix II' on June 10 2000, with an Alton–Salisbury–Alton special.
JOHN BIRD

The GWR 4-6-0 'Hall' class was a versatile 'mixed traffic' locomotive, an equal master of freight and passenger trains. On June 17 2000, No. 4936 *Kinlet Hall* pounds up the last few yards of Sapperton Bank on the Gloucester–Swindon 'Golden Valley' line.
GLEN BATTEN

The serried ranks of beach huts and bathers enjoying the water lend a traditional seaside atmosphere. LMS 'Black Five' No. 45407, posing as No. 45157 *The Glasgow Highlander*, climbs away from Paignton, Devon, with the 5.46pm Paignton–Exeter 'Dawlish Donkey' on August 12 2002. MARK WILKINS

When the sun is shining, the peat bogs on Rannoch Moor appear very attractive. On October 6 2002 a LNER partnership of 'K1' 2-6-0 No. 62005 (running as 62012) and 'B1' 4-6-0 No. 61264 (running as 61243 *Sir Harold Mitchell*) approach Corrour in the West Highlands.
JOHN COOPER-SMITH

The Settle & Carlisle line is noted for its rapidly-changing (and often poor) weather. On March 21 1987 LMS 'Jubilee' 4-6-0 No. 5593 *Kolhapur* departs from Garsdale with its S&C comeback tour. The locomotive was, during its British Railways career, a regular performer over the 72-miles line.
JOHN HUNT

Main line action as it should be. LMS 'Black Five' No. 45407, masquerading as scrapped classmate No. 45157 *The Glasgow Highlander*, races along at Gresson Lane, near Preston, with a train marking the 125th anniversary of the Settle & Carlisle line on May 1 2001.
BRIAN ROBBINS

▲ The heady days of summer are evoked as LNER 'A3' No. 4472 *Flying Scotsman* crosses the River Avon at Evesham, Worcestershire, on September 29 2001 with a Didcot-Worcester excursion.
MALCOLM RANIERI

► A very different view of Rannoch Moor's peat bogs, in the West Highlands, taken from the air on September 30 2000. In moody and damp conditions, LNER 'K1' 2-6-0 No. 62005 heads away from Corrour towards Rannoch with a special.
ED HURST

▶ Pride of the GWR fleet and mainstay of express passenger trains, GWR 'Castle' 4-6-0s continue to delight on the main line. On September 29 2001, No. 5029 *Nunney Castle* speeds past Grange Court, Gloucestershire, with a 'Severn Coast Express' crew-training run.
MALCOLM RANIERI

Proudly displaying 'The Inter-City' headboard, GWR 'King' 4-6-0 No. 6024 *King Edward I*, creates a spectacular display on October 6 2002 as it leaves Tyseley, West Midlands, with its Birmingham Snow Hill–Paddington special.
MALCOLM RANIERI

A solitary pine tree provides perfect framing for SR 'Merchant Navy' 4-6-2 No. 35028 *Clan Line* as it passes Tisbury with a London–Yeovil Junction special on October 3 1999. Bulleid 'Pacifics' were once regulars on this line, which once provided a route for the Southern Railway to Exeter, North Devon and Plymouth.
MARK WILKINS

Casting a perfect reflection on the still waters of Loch Lochy, LNER Thompson 'B1' 4-6-0 No. 61264 departs from Fort William with 'The Jacobite' for Mallaig on September 23 2002. JOHN LECK

In 1984, the first steam-hauled trains on the 'road to the isles' in 21 years attracted more passengers than BR had seats for. Against the unspoilt backdrop of the Ardnish headland, North British Railway 0-6-0 No. 673 *Maude*, crosses Loch Nam Uamh viaduct and prepares to attack the 1-in-48 Beasdale Bank on May 28 1984. JOHN COOPER-SMITH

The first locomotive reportedly to reach 100mph was GWR 4-4-0 No. 3440 *City of Truro* in 1904 on Wellington Bank, Somerset. In preservation *City of Truro* returned to the main line in late 1985 and following an appeal by *Steam Railway* magazine in 2001, is returning to steam in 2004, to mark the centenary of its record run. On May 3 1992, the venerable 4-4-0 passes Kingsbury, Warwickshire, on the Derby-Birmingham line bound for London Paddington.
MALCOLM RANIERI

For eight seasons until 1988, BR ran summer steam-hauled specials from York to Scarborough. In the third year, BR '9F' 2-10-0 No. 92220 *Evening Star*, the last steam locomotive built by BR, waits to leave York with the August 4 1983 'Scarborough Spa Express'. The '9F' made its final main line runs in 1988.
JOHN COOPER-SMITH

A WORLD away

Little survives of the Hedjaz Railway, famously attacked by Lawrence of Arabia, linking Damascus (Syria) and Ma'an (Jordan), but steam soldiers on in this inhospitable landscape. On September 22 2001 1956-built HSP 2-8-2 No. 71 works past a cemetery in the suburbs of Amman, Jordan, heading for Qasir with a freight.
JOHN HUNT

The steam railway was born in Britain, but was also one of our most significant gifts to the world. The creation of many modern countries as we know them today – the United States and India to name but two – would have been impossible without the 'iron road' that bound them together.

After the steam age drew to an end in this country at the close of the 1960s, some people started to look more keenly at what was on offer abroad.

Many countries kept the steam locomotive far longer than in its motherland, although the tide of dieselisation advanced quickly. By the beginning of the 21st Century working steam looked certain to face worldwide extinction within just a few years.

Currently only China is still a significant user of steam. With its large coal reserves and cheap labour, China was even still building steam locomotives until just a few years ago. But even here, steam is in full retreat. Who knows how much longer it may last?

The Khyber Pass, connecting Afghanistan and Pakistan is one of the most hostile places on earth, and its railway was built to serve the military during times of war; the idea to build it was conceived in 1878 during the second Afghan war. Trains climbing the pass are top-and-tailed due to the need to reverse at numerous 'zig-zags' used to gain height. British-built locomotives are used, the 'HGS' 2-8-0s and 'SGS' 0-6-0s, the latter are very similar to Great Central Railway 'Pom-Poms'. On December 29 1978 a pair of 'SGSs', Nos. 2487 and 2369, approach the start of the pass in the desert landscape at Jamrud, with the Fridays-only Peshawar-Landi Kotal.
LES NIXON

▶ It's early morning at Bridge Four near Aobaogou (Baotou), China, on December 29 2000 as a pair of 'QJ' 2-10-2s, banked by a third, attack the climb with a northbound goods.
MIKE TYACK.

Even in China, main line steam is becoming ever rarer as diesels take over. On the JiTong Railway, 'QJ' 2-10-2s Nos. 6110 and 7040 forge through the Jingpeng Pass near Galadesitai on February 1 2002.
PETER SKELTON

▶ Although regular main line steam in the former USSR finished by the 1990s, Russia has a huge strategic reserve of steam locomotives, which is only now starting to be dismantled. Many of the engines are massive freight types, such as these two 'L' 2-10-0s.
TONY STREETER

▼ A spectacular scene, blessed with the lucky combination of a clear blue sky, no wind and a foot of fresh snow. This was the sight that greeted the photographer in the Ukraine on February 28 2001, when visiting the Carpathian Mountains. Russian 'Er' and 'Em' 0-10-0s Nos. 735-72 and 797-86 work a special freight on the Rakhov-Delyatin line near Yasinya.
DAVID RODGERS

► Hear that lonesome whistle blow! On the Heber Valley Railroad, Utah, USA, Union Pacific 2-8-0 No. X-618 thunders past with a short freight in March 2002.
STUART LOVELL

▼ Despite the comedy that the 'Carry On' team portrayed, the Khyber Pass journey has never been one to undertake lightly. For five miles in its central portion, the pass becomes a twisting 600ft-wide defile hemmed in by precipitous 1,000ft high cliffs of limestone and slate. It is a desolate and hostile place where summer temperatures reach 48 degrees Celsius. British-built 'HGS' 2-8-0s Nos. 2216 and 2306 climb the 1-in-33 grade in the Pass on December 30 1998. The signal to the left of the picture shows where the line continues its climb on the next 'zig-zag'.
MAURICE BURNS

At first light on January 21 1999, China Rail's 'QJ' 2-10-2s Nos. 6760 and 7040 get underway near Jingpeng with an eastbound freight. The freezing temperatures and still air make for this impressive exhaust of condensing steam.
MIKE TYACK

SUNRISE, SUNSET

The steam railway used to be a 24 hour, seven day a week operation – as busy or busier at night than during the day. Whilst for today's steam railways that's no longer true, especially in winter trains often still run at the time of sunset – and just occasionally for sunrise too.

It can prove a challenge for photographers, but the combination of low sun, cold weather and steam can also lead to spectacular pictures. That's why clear winter's days have become firm favourites for those looking to create spectacular images.

At these times of day though planning and timing are everything, and if a train runs just a minute or two early or late, a picture can be ruined. It takes patience, persistence and skill to get it right.

All praise then, for those who do get it right at a time when most of us have packed away our cameras...

The sky is devoid of vapour trails from aircraft and the dying rays of the sun simply pick out a few small clouds and provide a wonderful backdrop for LMS '8F' 2-8-0 No. 48151 as it leaves Appleby, Cumbria, for Carlisle on November 26 1988. Autumn remains one of the best times of year for stunning pictures on the ever-popular Settle & Carlisle line.
LES NIXON

At the end of a glorious day, LMS '5MT' 4-6-0 No. 45407 crosses Whalley Arches, Lancashire, with its returning Carlisle-Manchester special on May 1 2001.
ED HURST

◄ As the sun dips below the horizon, the temperature has already started to drop and the fog is rolling in across the low lying land as LBSCR 'A1X' No. 2678 departs from Rolvenden, Kent & East Sussex Railway, at the start of its climb to Tenterden on February 15 2001.
ROBERT FALCONER

▼ The weak glow of the late afternoon sun relieves an almost monochromatic scene on December 28 2000 as LNER 'V2' 2-6-2 No. 60800 *Green Arrow* works northbound across Ribblehead Viaduct, North Yorkshire, with its Crewe–Carlisle 'Cumbrian Mountain Express'.
PAUL HEPPER

◀ Memories of the Eastern Region are awoken on the Great Central Railway (Nottingham) near Ruddington as LNER 'B1' 4-6-0 No. 61264, posing as No. 61248 *Geoffrey Gibbs*, glints in the low evening light shortly before sunset on May 4 2002. These locomotives, designed by Edward Thompson, had clean, simple lines and were the equivalent of the more prolific LMS 'Black Five'. In total 410 were built from 1942–51; today just two survive in preservation.
ALAN BARNES

▼ Catching the last rays of the evening light on August 26 2001, BR Standard '4MT' 2-6-0 No. 76079 drifts past Cockwood Harbour, Devon, with the return leg of its 'Tones Trotter' Exeter-Totnes-Exeter railtour.
BRIAN ROBBINS

All is at peace in the Worth Valley as 'Jinty' 0-6-0T No. 47279 heads towards Ingrow with a train from Keighley, just before the sun sets on January 4 2003.
PETER VAN CAMPENHOUT

A 'Westerner' a long way from home as visiting GWR 2-8-0T No. 4247 heads for Leicester North, Great Central Railway, with a train from Loughborough Central on January 19. The telegraph pole, now with just a single wire strung from it, is a reminder of a different age, when communication was by the beats of block instruments in a signalbox.
JOHN MARRIOTT

On November 3 2001, the last of the day's light picks out a country branch line freight heading home. South Devon Railway-based GWR 0-6-0 pannier tank No. 5786 passes Riverford.
PETER DOEL

With the last of the day's light picking out the locomotive's details, LNER 'B1' 4-6-0 No. 61264, making a brief visit to the Midland Railway, Derbyshire, crosses Butterley Reservoir on October 28 2001. Although an LNER design by Edward Thompson, many of the class were built by BR; 61264 however, was delivered in 1947, the year before nationalisation.
NICK HARRISON

Always a freight depot serving the extensive steel and coal industry around Barrow Hill, Derbyshire, the old 'Staveley Midland' shed yard comes alive on the evening of July 13 2001 with no fewer than five locomotives. From left to right are: BR '9F' 2-10-0 No. 92203, LNER 'B12' 4-6-0 No. 61572, LMS '1F' 0-6-0T No. 41708, LNER 0-4-0T 'Y7' No. 68088 and Hunslet 'Austerity' 0-6-0ST No. 68005.
ROBERT FALCONER

If the train had run just two minutes later, this picture could not have been taken, for the sun is just about to vanish beneath the horizon on January 27 2001. The tender of 1911-built GCR '04' 2-8-0 No. 63601 '04' obscures the sun as it heads south, approaching Quorn & Woodhouse station on the Great Central Railway, Leicestershire, with the 4pm Loughborough Central-Leicester North.
ROBIN BOYLE

Unusually facing downhill, the National Railway Museum's LNER 'V2' 2-6-2 No. 60800 *Green Arrow*, crosses the River Irwell with the 3pm Rawtenstall-Bury, East Lancashire Railway, on January 13 2001. The locomotive was named after a high-speed freight service introduced by the LNER on which the three-cylinder Gresley-designed 'V2s' were used.
BRIAN DOBBS

▲ It's the end of the day and a lucky coincidence on the Gloucestershire Warwickshire Railway sees the final rays of sun illuminate BR '9F' 2-10-0 No. 92203 *Black Prince* as it leaves Winchcombe with a train for Toddington on December 30 2000.
MALCOLM RANIERI

◄ A moody scene at Rawtenstall, East Lancashire Railway, on February 17 2001 as LMS '2MT' 2-6-0 No. 46441 takes water in the dying moments of daylight. The 12-mile line is popular with photographers, especially in the winter, and is one of only a handful of railways which run every weekend through the year.
JOHN LECK

The slowly fading light reflects in the low tide on March 30 2002 as LMS '8F' 2-8-0 No. 48151 heads across Arnside Viaduct, on the Cumbrian coast, with the return working of its Carnforth-Ravenglass excursion.
JOHN LECK

► A ghostly trail is left by the tail lamp on the rear of the 3.30pm Loughborough Central-Rothley, headed by Robinson '04' 2-8-0 No. 63601, as it passes through Quorn & Woodhouse station non-stop on December 18 2002.
JOHN MARRIOTT

▼ The sun has just dipped below the horizon on January 19 2002 at Diggle, near Manchester, creating a gentle warm glint on Riddles 'Mogul' No. 76079 heading for Manchester with a special from Huddersfield.
JOHN COOPER-SMITH

▲ Steam is now a rare visitor to the Cumbrian Coast Line, with its many low viaducts crossing rivers feeding the sea. On March 30 2002 against a gentle evening sky, LMS '8F' 2-8-0 No. 48151, built at Crewe as part of the war effort in 1942, glints as its crosses Arnside Viaduct with its returning Carnforth-Ravenglass excursion.
MICHAEL DENHOLM

◄ After the train's gone, peace returns to Damems station on January 11 2003. As the sun sinks, LMS '3F' 0-6-0T No. 47279 pulls away with the 3pm service to Oxenhope, Keighley & Worth Valley Railway.
EDDIE BOBROWSKI

▶ The sun has only just come up at the East Lancashire Railway and the cold conditions create a sharp, crisp, exhaust from BR Standard '4MT' 2-6-0 No. 76079 as it heads for Rawtenstall at Burrs on December 2 2001, with a three-coach 'local'.
BRIAN DOBBS

▼ Night is about to fall as newly-restored BR Standard '4MT' No. 80151 approaches Horsted Keynes, Bluebell Railway, with a 'Santa Special' on December 9 2001. Of the 155 Standard '4MT' 2-6-4 tanks built (between 1951–57), 15 have been saved from scrap and many of them have been restored to working order.
ED HURST

In only one minute's time the sun will have set and darkness descended. A last striking burst of sun heralds a final farewell for the day in this vision of sunset and steam at Barrow Hill Roundhouse, Derbyshire, on July 12 2002. Highlighted for the last time this day are, from the left, LNER 'Y7' 0-4-0T No. 68088, GWR '57XX' 0-6-0PT No. 7754 and MR '1F' 0-6-0T No. 41708.
ED HURST

Water laying in the fields reflects the setting sun at Burrs, East Lancashire Railway, on February 6 2002 as LMS '2MT' 2-6-0 No. 46441 heads north with a parcels train. Once a common scene all over the north west, such sights are now confined largely to the 12-mile preserved line.
JOHN LECK

DOUBLE headed

What could be more magnificent than a steam locomotive rolling majestically through the landscape? Well, how about a pair?

Traditionally locomotives were used in pairs ('double-headed') when trains were too heavy to use just one. That naturally often meant that it happened where the railway is at its steepest - and the scenery therefore at its most spectacular.

On many lines, locomotives were kept at strategic places especially to double-head (or in some cases 'bank', or help them from the rear). Some designs of locomotive were even produced especially for the purpose.

Double-heading these days is relatively rare, not least because of the increased cost of using two locomotives instead of one. But where it does happen, it can bring a double thrill to the senses – and a great reminder of how things, sometimes, used to be.

With their exhausts in almost perfect symmetry, and both engines blowing off steam, an LMS duo of Hughes 'Crab' 2-6-0 No. 42745 and Stanier 4-6-0 'Black Five' No. 45337 (posing as No. 45156 *Ayrshire Yeomanry*) work across Summerseat Viaduct, East Lancashire Railway, with the 9am Bury-Rawtenstall on February 22 2001.
EDDIE BOBROWSKI

Creating a 1950s-style scene with their rake of red and cream BR Mk 1 coaches in tow, GWR 4-6-0s Nos. 4936 *Kinlet Hall* and 5029 *Nunney Castle* romp around the curves at Horse Cove, near Dawlish, Devon, bound for Penzance on April 7 2001. When Isambard Kingdom Brunel surveyed the section west of Exeter to Newton Abbot he had two choices, either to tackle the gradients of Dartmoor, or build a railway hugging the coast. His choice of the latter has been a public advertisement for the railway ever since.
PETER DOEL

▶ The drama of colliery steam is on show to full effect at the Foxfield Railway's July 21/22 2001 gala. Two of the Staffordshire line's plucky 0-4-0STs, Beyer Peacock No. 1827 and Robert Heath No. 6, are almost enveloped in smoke and steam as they prepare to do battle with the 1-in-19 Foxfield bank on a train of coal wagons.
ROBERT BRITTLE

▼ A Safari Silhouette as GWR pannier tank 0-6-0 No. 5764 and Port Talbot Railway 0-6-0ST No. 813 trundle round Safari Curve, named after the adjacent game park, near Bewdley, Severn Valley Railway, on December 28 2002.
MALCOLM RANIERI

The low winter sun creates a sculptured effect in the exhausts from BR Standard Class '4MT' 4-6-0 No. 75027 and BR Standard '9F' 2-10-0 No. 92240 as they charge past Treemans, Bluebell Railway, on November 13 2000.
ED HURST

Sparkling with polished brass and copper as only Great Western Railway locomotives can, 4-6-0s Nos. 4936 *Kinlet Hall* and 5029 *Nunney Castle* bring their heavy train across Coombe Viaduct, Saltash, Cornwall, with 'The Royal Duchy' from Penzance to Taunton on April 16 2001. In the background is the River Tamar, with Plymouth's Devonport just out of the picture.
BRIAN ROBBINS

STEAM in industry

Industry spawned the steam locomotive and – in Britain at least – industry was where it ended its working life. Steam gave way to diesel and electric engines on the main lines in the 1950s and 1960s, but in industry the last of the old workhorses clung on into the 1980s.

Often neglected by enthusiasts at the time, the little engines that kept industry on the move were as important to the country as their more glamorous cousins, and many hundreds of industrial steam locomotives have survived.

Many are in museums or see occasional use at steam railways, although a few preserved lines – such as the Middleton, Tanfield and Foxfield Railways – are former industrial railways, proud of their heritage. In recent years, preservationists have also taken industrial locomotives back to working industrial plants, to recreate the days when they worked there 'for real'. These days, photographers are kinder on the industrial machine and this chapter celebrates the best of the little locomotives that helped keep the wheels of industry moving...

Back in the environment in which it, and so many other Peckett 0-4-0STs were built for, but dwarfed by its surroundings, No. 2087 pounds through Workington steelworks on September 14 2002 with a train of ballast wagons.
ED HURST

◀ Dwarfed by mountains of newly-imported gypsum, Lancashire and Yorkshire Railway 'Pug' 0-4-0ST No. 51218 hustles its short freight along the dockside at Workington Harbour on March 30 2001. Built specifically for working in docks and other industrial sites with sharp curves and where larger locomotives would not fit, some of the 57-strong class, built from 1891-1910, survived into the 1960s. Two examples were saved for preservation.
DAVID WILCOCK

▲ Scuttling amongst dockside cranes at Goole docks on March 15 2003 is Lancashire & Yorkshire Railway 'Pug' 0-4-0ST No. 51218, running as former Goole-based engine No. 51241, serving as a reminder of the work these engines used to do.
ED HURST

Strong backlighting picks out the detail in snow laying in the fields and the combined exhaust of 1879-built Beyer Peacock and 1886-built Robert Heath 0-4-0STs. They storm up the 1-in-19 Foxfield Bank, Foxfield Railway, Staffordshire, in the early afternoon sun on December 29 2000.
BRIAN DOBBS

▶ Sand on the rails is testimony to the steepness of the 1-in-25, stiffening to 1-in-19 for a short while, of Foxfield Bank, Foxfield Railway, Staffordshire. On July 29 1995 during a steam gala 1886-built Robert Heath 0-4-0ST No. 6 and 1914-built Peckett 0-4-0ST *Lion*, clamber up the climb with a coal train for Dilhorne Park, from Foxfield Colliery. The railway has won a Lottery grant with which it has bought the disused colliery.
ROBIN STEWART SMITH

▼ Nowadays a rarity in Britain, a working quarry with its own railway; Barrington, Cambridgeshire, is normally diesel-worked. But occasionally photographers have taken steam locomotives to the location where they once ruled supreme. On September 6 2001, Avonside 0-4-0 saddle tank *Barrington* returned to the quarry where it once worked. It was joined by another almost identical 0-4-0ST from the same Bristol locomotive builder, the bright blue *Dora*, which was loaned from the Rutland Railway Museum. *Dora* contrasts sharply with the almost lunar-like landscape.
MALCOLM RANIERI

FREIGHT
on the line

The steam railway was created to move goods – when Trevithick's first successful locomotive 'Penydarren' ushered in the modern age by shuffling along a few miles of the Penydarren Tramroad, it was to move freight not people.

Right until the end of steam, goods were the railway's prime earner, if not the main focus of publicity.

Unlike the relatively fast and glamorous passenger trains, goods trains were slow, and often moved at night. In contrast to the famous high-stepping polished machines to haul the prestige expresses, goods engines developed into heavy sloggers, with lots of small wheels to provide plenty of grip. But moving goods wasn't just about heavy trains – it was as much about occasional wagons collected from branch line stations as long coal trains rumbling along the main lines.

When BR's last steam locomotive, '9F' 2-10-0 No. 92220 *Evening star* was built at Swindon in 1960, steam locomotive design ended where it had begun – to haul freight.

These days Britain's surviving steam railways rely almost completely on passengers, but many have restored goods wagons in order to run 'demonstration' trains. The pictures on these pages show just how well they've done...

One of preservation's pioneers is the Ffestiniog Railway, now one of the finest steam railways the UK has to offer. Originally built to serve the enormous slate mines at Blaenau Ffestiniog, one of its early locomotives, 1863-built George England 0-4-0STT *Prince* approaches Campbell's Platform with a train of empty slate wagons on November 9 2001.
ED HURST

► Like most railways, the Welshpool & Llanfair Light Railway was built at the turn of the last century to serve farmers in the rolling hills from the mid-Wales town. Evoking memories of the line as a freight railway, Beyer Peacock 0-6-0T No. 822 *The Earl* is near Sylfaen with a goods train on December 3 2000.
ED HURST

▼ Doing the work it was intended for when built in 1911 by the Great Central Railway at its Gorton, Manchester workshops, '04' No. 63601 powers away from Loughborough, Leicestershire on July 28 2001 with a rake of 16-ton mineral wagons. Running on the present-day Great Central Railway, an eight-mile section of the former Sheffield-London main line, the locomotive was restored by the railway following a fund-raising appeal by *Steam Railway* magazine.
MALCOLM RANIERI

◀ There's still a touch of snow on the top of Cadair Idris in the far distance as Corris Railway No. 4 and a train of Corris stock wends its way along the Talyllyn Railway on February 24. During its pre-preservation days, in addition to the slate traffic for which it was built, this mid-Wales line served the small farming communities along its way up the valley.
TERRY EYRES

▼ The sun attempts to burn off the mist as LNER 'B1' 4-6-0 No. 61264 thrashes along the Great Central Railway's double-track main line near Swithland Reservoir on March 12 2002 with a mixed postal and parcels train.
ED HURST

Recreating a classic scene, a daily occurrence during the line's working days (although with locomotives and stock much more decrepit than today). A mixed goods, headed by London Brighton & South Coast Railway 'Terrier' 0-6-0T No. 32678, runs through scrubland reclaimed from marshes near Wittersham Road, Kent & East Sussex Railway on February 23 2002.
ED HURST

Despite its diminutive size, this 1921-built 0-4-2T was designed as a freight slogger for hauling slate trains on the Corris Railway, mid-Wales. Now at home on the nearby Talyllyn Railway it is in charge of a small mixed goods at Brynglas on May 4 1998. Both railways shared the gauge of 2ft 3in, found nowhere else in Britain.
TERRY EYRES

Standing out in sharp relief against a cloudless sky as the sun starts to set, LNER 'B1' 4-6-0 No. 61264 and its short freight train are in perfect silhouette between Sheringham and Weybourne on May 31 2002. This was the North Norfolk Railway's 'Jubilee Week' to mark the Golden Jubilee of the coronation of HM Queen Elizabeth II.
ED HURST

STEAM
in its
surroundings

Dwarfed by the stunning Cumbrian scenery of the Lake District, LMS Fairburn 2-6-4T No. 42073 heads for Lakeside on the Lakeside and Haverthwaite Railway. The still waters of Windermere reflect the train as it works along the 3.5 miles line.
PETER DOEL

More than anything that went before them, the railways shaped and influenced Britain's landscape - but they still became a part of it. Soon the branch line train rolling gently through the countryside, the heavy express storming steep main line gradients, or freight curving its way through the blackened surroundings of an industrial town were as much part of the scene as the churches and houses that had stood for generations.

Memories were made of glimpses of locomotives at the end of streets, through windows or maybe just as smudges of smoke in the distance.

Fortunately, at Britain's steam railways you can still recreate those memories. What's more, dedicated steam landscape photographers paint the railways onto the canvas of the surrounding country, so we can bring them into your living room...

► Turning the clock back around 130 years is this vista at the Midland Railway, Butterley Derbyshire, with two 1860s vintage steam locomotives. At Swanwick Junction on May 8 2001, to the right Furness Railway 0-4-0 No. 20 dating from 1863, passes Midland Railway 2-4-0 No. 158A dating from 1866, with a train of vintage stock.
MALCOLM RANIERI

▼ Days of stopping trains on the former GCR main line are remembered as LNER 'B1' 4-6-0 No. 61264 rounds the curve at Kinchley Lane, Great Central Railway, with a train for Leicester on February 25 2001.
NICK HARRISON

◀ With a matching rake of GWR stock in tow, Great Western Railway 2-6-2T No. 4144 departs from Bewdley, Severn Valley Railway, with a train for Kidderminster, during the 16-mile line's 'Branch Line Gala' on March 4 2001. The 2-6-2 'Prairie' design was most commonly to be found on the GWR, where they worked freight and passenger trains on branch lines, and commuter trains. This locomotive, built at Swindon in 1946, was one of the 180-strong '5101' class. They were a 1929 development by Collett of Churchward's '3100' class.
MALCOLM RANIERI

▼ The landscape is briefly disturbed by the perfect exhaust of LMS 'Crab' 2-6-0 No. 42765 as it rolls into Irwell Vale station, East Lancashire Railway, with the 10am Bury Bolton Street–Rawtenstall on January 11 2003.
NIGEL VALENTINE

The Ffestiniog Railway in the winter. Crossing the Cob at Porthmadog – a man-made causeway across the tidal marshes – on February 16 2002 is 1893-built Hunslet 2-4-0STT *Linda* with slate empties from the harbour town.
JOHN LECK

▲ Steam trails in the cold morning air of December 2 2001 are matched by steam from Kidderminster's sugar processing factory as the beet campaign is in full swing. Meanwhile, LMS 'Black Five' 4-6-0 No. 45110 heads an empty stock train into Bewdley Tunnel, Severn Valley Railway. At the rear of the train are GWR 0-6-0PT No. 5764 and GWR 0-4-0ST No. 813.
RALPH WARD

► The epitome of a British Railways branch line as BR Standard '4MT' 2-6-4T No. 80002 crosses Mytholmes Viaduct with the 4.45pm Keighley-Oxenhope, Keighley & Worth Valley Railway, on March 31 1997. The five-mile line never ran any further than its Oxenhope terminus and is extremely rare in being preserved in its entirety.
DAVID RODGERS

▶ In crisp winter light, SR 'West Country' 4-6-2 No. 34027 *Taw Valley* departs from Quorn & Woodhouse station, Great Central Railway, Leicestershire, with a morning train for Loughborough Central on January 28 2001. It is painted maroon in connection with a promotional tour for the *Harry Potter* books, but has since returned to British Railways standard Brunswick green.
PETER DOEL

▼ Ivatt '2MT' No. 41312 paid a visit to the Great Central Railway in October and in the evening of October 28, disguised as classmate No. 41301, heads along the GCR's double-track main line at Woodthorpe. The colour-light signal is based on an original LNER design.
MALCOLM RANIERI

Bathed in early morning sunshine, this clean, crisp view recreates summer Saturday scenes in the 1950s. Then every available engine was pressed into service, including occasionally 2-10-0 War Department freight engines such as No. 90775, which departs from Loughborough, Great Central Railway, on July 28 2002.
MALCOLM RANIERI

◄ Accelerating across the moorland at Moorgates, North Yorkshire Moors Railway, on October 31 2002 is LMS 'Black Five' No. 45337 with a Grosmont–Pickering train. Behind the locomotive is a Gresley teak coach, one of a number restored at the railway.
JOHN LECK

▲ Moody weather provides an ominous backdrop to tiny Hunslet 0-4-0ST *Lilla* as it attacks the 1-in-76 climb to Tanygrisiau, Ffestiniog Railway, North Wales on November 2 2002. Built in 1891 to a design commonly known as 'The Quarry Hunslets' these diminutive locomotives were noted for spending their days working in the giant North Wales slate quarries, when they were not provided with cabs.
DAVID WILCOCK

► Once an industrial railway, built more than 125 years ago to haul minerals, the 15-inch gauge Ravenglass and Eskdale Railway is now a leading tourist attraction, taking visitors from the coast at Ravenglass through seven miles of wonderful Lake District scenery. On February 12 2001 *River Mite* climbs away from The Green station with the 1.50pm Ravenglass-Dalegarth.
JOHN HUNT

▼ Ffestiniog Railway 'Double Fairlie' 0-4-4-0T *David Lloyd George* passes Llyn Ystridau and approaches Moelwyn Tunnel with the 3.15pm Blaenau Ffestiniog-Porthmadog on August 29 2001. Despite its elderly appearance, the locomotive was built as recently as 1992, but follows the design of the railway's original 1870s 'Double Fairlies', effectively two locomotives stuck back-to-back.
JOHN HUNT

Lost in the timeless hills of Yorkshire, LMS 'Jinty' 0-6-0T No. 47279 climbs from Oakworth towards Haworth, Keighley & Worth Valley Railway, on January 4 2003.
PETER VAN CAMPENHOUT

98

◄ The bare trees stand starkly in the cold, while steam heat warms the passengers of the seven-coach Leicester North–Loughborough train hauled by SR 'Pacific' No. 34027 *Taw Valley* on the Great Central Railway, Leicestershire, on December 29 2000. At this time the locomotive was painted maroon for promotion work in connection with the *Harry Potter* books, yet the strong winter sunlight hides its unusual colours.
RALPH WARD

Visiting the Gloucestershire Warwickshire Railway from the Llangollen Railway, GWR 4-6-0 No. 7822 *Foxcote Manor* departs from Winchcombe with a train for Gotherington in late winter sunshine on March 9 2002.
MALCOLM RANIERI

◄ Set amongst the distinctive North Yorkshire Moors, the railway which takes its name from the National Park where it is based, the Pickering–Grosmont line offers a strong North Eastern Railway flavour. LNER Peppercorn 'A2' 4-6-2 No. 60532 *Blue Peter* leaves Levisham with the 12.50pm Grosmont–Pickering on October 31 2001.
JOHN HUNT

▼ Memories of main line summers are evoked near Harman's Cross, Swanage Railway, as SR 'Merchant Navy' 4-6-2 No. 35027 *Port Line* heads for Norden on September 14 2002 during the Dorset line's steam gala.
PAUL BLOWFIELD

On one of its final days in traffic before its ten-year boiler certificate expired on New Year's Eve, requiring a compulsory overhaul, BR Standard Class '2MT' 2-6-0 No. 78022 meets the setting sun head on. It climbs through an industrial landscape at Ingrow, Keighley & Worth Valley Railway, West Yorkshire, with the 2.50pm Keighley–Oxenhope on December 27 2000.
EDDIE BOBROWSKI

▲ The first buds of spring are starting to appear on April 11 2001 as Beyer Peacock 2-4-0T No. 10 *G.H. Wood*, with matching newly-outshopped red and cream coaches, departs from Castletown, Isle of Man Steam Railway, with the 2pm Douglas-Port Erin.
DOUG BIRMINGHAM

◄ The River Banwy looks peaceful and gently flowing in this scene on April 7 2002, however after heavy rain it would be impossible to stand in this position and the bridge, over which 0-6-0T No. 822 passes, has been seriously damaged on two occasions in the last 40 years by storm waters. However, the Welshpool & Llanfair Light Railway has always been a survivor, thanks to the efforts of its dedicated volunteers and supporters.
MALCOLM RANIERI

Exhaust steam combines with mist hanging in the Esk Valley and smoke from chimneys as Lambton 0-6-2T No. 29 heads towards Goathland with a 'Santa Special' from Grosmont, North Yorkshire Moors Railway, on December 2 2001.
JOHN HUNT

The sort of conditions that photographers dream about, snow, sun and cold conditions. BR Standard '4MT' 2-6-0 No. 76079 disturbs a landscape of newly-fallen snow as it leaves Ramsbottom, East Lancashire Railway, with the second train of the day, the 11am Bury Bolton Street–Rawtenstall on December 30 2001.
MIKE TAYLOR

Laying an almost perfect trail of clean white exhaust, BR Standard '9F' 2-10-0 No. 92212 climbs the 1.25 miles 1-in-100 Eardington Bank on the Severn Valley Railway, Worcestershire, with the 1.15pm Kidderminster-Bridgnorth on December 28 2000.
ROBIN BOYLE

◀ What could easily be a 1960s Birmingham semi-fast is re-created as GWR '5101' class 'Prairie' No. 4141 leaves Rothley with a train for Loughborough Central, Great Central Railway on February 1 2003.
MALCOLM RANIERI

▶ Low winter lighting glints on the side tanks of LMS 2-6-4T '4MT' No. 42073 as it rounds the curve out of Newby Bridge, Lakeside & Haverthwaite Railway, on November 16 2002.
PETER VAN CAMPENHOUT

▼ Foggy conditions add to the late-BR steam era feel as LMS 'Black Five' 4-6-0s Nos. 45407 (running as 45157 *The Glasgow Highlander*) and 45337 (running as 45156 *Ayrshire Yeomanry*) pass Burrs, during the East Lancashire Railway's gala on January 28 2001.
ED HURST

You can almost feel the cold in this picture, which could almost be a 1950s Christmas extra. Forcing the snow off the railhead as it advances south, 'WD' 2-10-0 No. 90775 roars away from Woodthorpe, Great Central Railway, en route to Leicester North on January 4 2003.
RALPH WARD

▲ 'She's full!' Peckett 0-4-0 saddle tank No. 2142 fills its tank at the Telford Steam Railway, Shropshire, on October 26 2002.
ALAN BARNES

▶ Early morning near Oakworth on the Keighley & Worth Valley Railway during its gala on October 13 2002 finds BR Standard '4MT' 2-6-0 No. 76079 climbing the half-mile 1-in-60 gradient with the 9am Ingrow-Oxenhope. Its exhaust hangs without disturbance in the still morning air, betraying its route up the valley.
MIKE TAYLOR

◄ Great Eastern Railway magic in this period scene at Weybourne station, North Norfolk Railway on January 18 2003 as 'B12' 4-6-0 No. 61572 arrives with a westbound train. Meanwhile, Great Eastern Railway 'J15' 0-6-0 No. 65462 plods into the station with a short freight.
ED HURST

▼ Cold conditions and hardly any wind leaves the exhaust hanging in the air on December 28 2000 as GCR Class '04' 2-8-0 No. 63601 departs from Loughborough Central, Great Central Railway, with a train for Leicester North.
LES NIXON

▼ This could almost be a 1950s BR Western Region scene, but is in fact WR 4-6-0 'Manor' No. 7821 *Odney Manor* at Swithland, Great Central Railway, on December 8 2001. One of the last GWR 4-6-0 types, 30 locomotives designed by C.B. Collett for secondary main lines, were built from 1938 into BR days in 1950. Nine survive into preservation and all have been returned to steam at some time during the last 35 years.
MALCOLM RANIERI

▶ In a display of raw power, Gresley-designed 'V2' No. 60800 *Green Arrow* roars away from Loughborough Central, Great Central Railway, on September 1 2002 with 'The South Yorkshireman' bound for Leicester North. Owned by the York-based National Railway Museum, the 'V2' acts as a roving ambassador for the Science Museum offshoot.
MALCOLM RANIERI

◀ Morning glory, Western Region style, as GWR 'Manor' 4-6-0 No. 7821 *Ditcheat Manor* raises ghosts of inter-regional services in the 1950s near Quorn & Woodhouse, Great Central Railway, as it accelerates southwards on December 18 2002.
ALAN BARNES

▼ Steam in winter at the Severn Valley Railway, Worcestershire. It's December 2 2000 and BR Standard Class '9F' 2-10-0 No. 92212 waits at Kidderminster Town with a Santa Special for Arley, dwarfing GWR 0-6-0 pannier tank No. 7714 as it departs with a similar service. The last GWR pannier tanks of this design were built in 1949; just five years later the first '9Fs' emerged – such a contrast could not be stronger.
MICHAEL DENHOLM

◄ A vivid impression at Horsenden Crossing, Buckinghamshire, as Great Western Railway 0-4-2T '14XX' No. 1420 passes on January 7 2001. The 1933-built locomotive was visiting the Chinnor & Princes Risborough Railway from its normal home on the South Devon Railway.
GEOFF SILCOCK

A Christmas card scene on the Bluebell Railway, West Sussex as London Brighton & South Coast Railway 'Terrier' 0-6-0T No. W8 *Freshwater*, on loan from the Isle of Wight Steam Railway, pilots LBSCR 'E4' 0-6-2T No. 473 *Birch Grove* with the 1.30pm Horsted Keynes–Sheffield Park on December 30 2000. The 'Terrier', built in 1876, pre-dates the Billington-designed Class 'E4' by 12 years.
MIKE ESAU

▲ The late afternoon sun glistens on the freshly-fallen snow as BR '9F' 2-10-0 No. 92203 *Black Prince* heads around Chicken Curve, Gloucestershire Warwickshire Railway, accelerating away from its Winchcombe stop with a train for Toddington. The locomotive is owned by David Shepherd, the artist well-known for his paintings of African wildlife.
JOHN CHALCRAFT

◄ Superpower on the Welshpool and Llanfair Light Railway is provided on August 31 2002 by Finnish 2-6-2T No. 5 *Orion*, which prepares to leave Llanfair Caerenion with the 6.25pm to Welshpool. The open end balconies of the coaches are a particular, and unique, attraction to this 2ft 6in gauge railway.
MICHAEL DENHOLM

This is the sort of railway scene that many people still remember; a large locomotive, neatly tended station and a forest of semaphore signals. This splendid vision is thanks to the hard work of volunteers and staff on the North Yorkshire Moors Railway. The rousing scene at Grosmont on February 14 2002 is completed by War Department 2-10-0 No. 90775 as its leaves the station with a train for Pickering, the line's southern terminus.
JOHN LECK

◄ Creating its own smog in Norfolk, visiting LNER 'B1' 4-6-0 No. 61264 (running as 61170) completes an almost monochrome image as it drifts through Weybourne station, North Norfolk Railway, on May 31 2003.
ROBERT FALCONER

◄ Steam, sun, snow and mist combine as LMS 'Jinty' 0-6-0 No. 47357 crosses Butterley Reservoir, Midland Railway, Derbyshire, with the 11am Butterley–Hammersmith on January 1 2002.
MICK HOLLINGWORTH

▼ Autumn on the Great Central Railway, with lineside silver birch trees providing a foil for War Department 2-10-0 No. 90775, built in 1943, as it stomps away from Loughborough with a train for Leicester North on October 19 2002.
LES NIXON

Cosying up to each other, three 2ft-gauge locomotives provide a magical start to the day at Warren Wood shed, Bredgar & Wormshill Light Railway, Kent. From the left are Schwartzkopf 0-4-0WT No. 1 *Bronhilde*, Hunslet 0-4-0ST *Lady Joan* and Orenstein & Koppel 0-4-0WT No. 6 *Eigiau*.
ANDREW SMITH

Pride of the 'BIG FOUR' railways

Britain's railway system sprang up as hundreds of different uncoordinated railway companies, promoted by different people. This rash of independent lines soon started to consolidate naturally, but it was fairly slow. It was only after the First World War that the government pushed the process, in what became known as the 'Grouping'.

The result, from 1923, was the creation of four large railway companies covering the whole of Britain. These were the London Midland and Scottish, the London and North Eastern Railway, the Great Western Railway (a survivor from pre-grouping days) and the Southern Railway.

All the new companies had distinctive locomotive designs, and the 'Big Four' era was characterised by competition to be bigger, better and faster than the other companies. The result was many of the magnificent locomotives we still have in preservation today. This chapter celebrates the fine machines that were the work of the 'Big Four's' great designers...

It could almost be New England shed, Peterborough, in the 1950s, but this is Barrow Hill Roundhouse, near Chesterfield. In a superbly atmospheric scene, an LNER duo of 'V2' 2-6-2 No. 60800 *Green Arrow* and 'B1' 4-6-0 No. 61264 simmer under the yard lights outside the roundhouse on April 19 2002.
PETER SKELTON

▲ Early stars of the main line steam revival following BR's lifting of the steam ban in 1971 were this magnificent LNER duo of Gresley-designed locomotives. On September 13 1975 'V2' 2-6-2 No. 4771 *Green Arrow* and 'A3' 4-6-2 No. 4472 *Flying Scotsman* depart from York station, both in the LNER's most attractive apple green livery.
LES NIXON

▶ An evocative Great Western Railway scene at the single-platform Arley station, Severn Valley Railway, on March 19 2001 as 'Prairie' No. 4144, visiting from the Didcot Railway Centre, passes with a two coach local. Immediately behind the locomotive is a ventilated van, often used to carry perishables, such as milk churns.
COLIN BINCH

Looking every inch a main line, in truth this is the eight-miles Great Central Railway, Leicestershire, whose double track standard gauge steam-worked railway is unique in the world. On a clear, crisp December 28 2000, LNER 'B1' No. 61264 (which was rebuilt from a scrapyard wreck at the railway) accelerates towards Swithland Reservoir with a Loughborough Central-Leicester North train.
MALCOLM RANIERI

A scene reminiscent of 'Top Shed' at London King's Cross, as LNER 'Pacifics' Nos. 4498 *Sir Nigel Gresley*, No. 4472 *Flying Scotsman* and No. 4468 *Mallard* stand at London Marylebone on October 11 1986. This line up of the world's most famous locomotives was whilst BR was running a series of Sunday Luncheon trains from the London terminus to Stratford-upon-Avon.
GEOFF SILCOCK

An LMS interloper in GWR territory, although in reality each had running powers onto the other's tracks, and this scene is reminiscent of the Central Wales line, a line worked by 'Black Fives' in BR days. On April 8 2002, LMS 'Black Five' 4-6-0 No. 45110 departs under GWR signals from Bewdley, Severn Valley Railway.
MALCOLM RANIERI

Handsomely proportioned, the 70 Arthur Peppercorn-designed 'K1' class 'Moguls' were built from 1949-1950 and were amongst the final LNER 1-1 design locomotives to be built, although the lack of capacity post-war in the railway's own workshops meant that their construction was sub-contracted to the North British Locomotive Company of Glasgow, whose distinctive diamond-shaped builders plate is on the smokebox side. For many years a regular on the Fort William-Mallaig 'Jacobite' tourist trains, the sole-surviving 'K1' No. 62005 stands on shed at Fort William on July 19 2001.
JOHN HUNT

Go south for sunshine... the Southern Railway's slogan was validated on September 20 2001 when the Bluebell Railway, East Sussex, was blessed with perfect conditions for its pairing of Bullied 'Light Pacifics'. 'Battle of Britain' No. 34081 *92 Squadron* leads 'West Country' No. 21C123 *Blackmoor Vale* at Holywell. Built in 1948 and 1946 respectively, mechanically they are identical.
ED HURST

A brace of GWR 'Hall' class 4-6-0s, 1929-built Nos. 4936 *Kinlet Hall* and 1931-built 4965 *Rood Ashton Hall*, simmer adjacent to Tyseley Warwick Road signalbox, Tyseley Locomotive Works, on October 27 2000. When preserved *Rood Ashton Hall* was thought to be No. 4983 *Albert Hall*. However, during its restoration identity stampings on components confirmed that its identity had been swapped during its last overhaul at Swindon Works.
DEREK HUNTRISS

STEAM
byways

Away from the main lines, the steam railway took on a very different character. Country branch lines and secondary routes worked to a different, more relaxed rhythm, in tune with the communities they served. It wasn't unknown for trains to drop people off right outside their front doors, or for crews to pause to collect firewood to take home...

Yet with the explosion of private car ownership and bus services after the war, these railways were very quickly under threat and the Beeching report of 1963 spelt the end for many. It was this, and the simultaneous replacement of the steam locomotive, which sparked the steam preservation movement. By the end of that decade, revived steam railways were springing up all over the country, a process that has never stopped since.

Most were the former branch lines, so you can still enjoy the 'steam byway' today, even if - maybe - the train won't stop right outside your front door...

The elegant footbridge and architecture immediately place this picture in Scotland, and Caledonian Railway 0-6-0 No. 57566, built in 1899 at St Rollox works, Glasgow, completes the scene as it waits to leave Boat of Garten station, Strathspey Railway, on September 29 2000.
JOHN COOPER-SMITH

Climbing steep gradients and around sharp curves, the 2ft 6in gauge Welshpool & Llanfair Light Railway does exactly what narrow-gauge railways were built for, serving communities where a standard gauge railway would have been prohibitively expensive to build. Giving a good impression of the line in early BR days before its closure in 1956, 1902-built Beyer Peacock 0-6-0T No. 822 wends its way through mid-Wales countryside on April 7 2002.
ED HURST

▲ With snow and ice clinging to the lineside, GWR 0-6-0 pannier tank No. 1369, visiting from the South Devon Railway, shunts wagons at Bronwydd Arms station, Gwili Railway, on December 30 2000. Although similar in appearance to the hundreds of other 0-6-0PTs built by the GWR, this is the only survivor of the six-strong '1366' class, built in 1934 for dock shunting. At 35.75 tons, they were around 10 tons lighter than other versions and can be recognised by having outside, rather than inside, cylinders.
SIMON HOPKINS

◄ Strongly back-lit by low winter sun, the second train of the day on the three-mile Tanfield Railway, Tyne & Wear, hauled by 1923-built Hawthorn Leslie 0-6-0ST *Stagshaw* heads under Gibraltar Bridge on November 26 2000.
DAVE HEWITT

▲ Deep in the enchanting Royal Forest of Dean, Gloucestershire, Collett-designed GWR 0-6-0 '2251' class No. 3205 shuffles into Parkend station with a short pick-up goods train. This is now the northern section of the Dean Forest Railway and when this picture was taken on September 22 2001, work was continuing to re-open it to passenger trains.
ED HURST

► During the winter the Wareham-Swanage branch was a quiet, backwater affair, only coming alive with holidaymakers in the summer. In preservation it remains equally popular and the six-mile line retains its BR Southern Region flavour. On June 10 2001, the Dorset line saw BR Standard '4MT' 2-6-4T No. 80104 in service, departing from Harman's Cross.
ED HURST

Stirring memories of when the Severn Valley Railway was just another cross-country byway, with connecting branches to places such as Hartlebury and Cleobury Mortimer, a GWR auto-train approaches Bewdley, Worcestershire, from the south on March 5 2001. The locomotive, GWR 0-4-2T '14XX' No. 1420 loaned from the South Devon Railway, has been renumbered to represent 1417 for the day, and is married with a single auto-coach.
ED HURST

Near Berwyn, Llangollen Railway, on November 10 2002, GWR 0-6-0PT No. 7754 trundles through the Dee Valley with a two-coach 'local'. MALCOLM RANIERI

A rural byway if ever there was one, and a recreation of once common scenes across the lightly laid country lines that once criss-crossed East Anglia. It's July 19 2002 at the embryonic Mid-Suffolk Railway at Brockford as GER 'J15' 0-6-0 No. 65447, loaned from the North Norfolk Railway, rests for a moment.
MALCOLM RANIERI

155

The vintage charm of the Isle of Man Railway has been slightly dissipated since this picture was taken, following investment by its owner, the Manx Government, which has re-laid the track with new materials on clean ballast. On October 18 2001 Beyer Peacock 2-4-0T No. 11 *Maitland*, built in 1905, trundles past Ballagawne crossing, Colby.
MALCOLM RANIERI

NOCTURNE

The GWR engine shed at Didcot is the only original large engine shed, apart from Barrow Hill Roundhouse, open to the public in the UK. Better still it houses a unique collection of Great Western Railway locomotives, one of which is 0-6-0 pannier tank No. 3738, that stands alongside the shed in the rain on October 29 1999.
SIMON HOPKINS

All the visitors have gone home long ago, but it is at night that the steam railway is perhaps at its most atmospheric. It's also a time when the photographic challenges are greater, and exposure times are measured in seconds rather than the blink of an eye.

Despite this, the hours after darkness have become a favourite time for Britain's steam photographers, who increasingly organise elaborately staged night-time events to recapture the best of the railway at night. Who can blame them? In steam days the railway was as busy at night as during the day, and these days it is at night - when most general visitors are in bed - when the years fall away most convincingly. We hope you enjoy our selection of pictures during the quiet hours, when signal box bells ting out through the gloom, and locomotives gurgle gently to themselves on shed...

▲ A silent station with just LMS '4F' 0-6-0 No. 44422 and a single guard's van, running 'horse and cart' in railway parlance, pause at the attractive Cheddleton station, Churnet Valley Railway, in October 1997.
GEOFF LEE

► Visiting from the West Somerset Railway, 1934-built 'auto-pannier' No. 6412 recreates a GWR scene underneath the footbridge at Toddington, Gloucestershire Warwickshire Railway, on August 18 2001. Eventually the railway intends to extend northwards (the direction of this picture) to reach the Cotswold town of Broadway, and maybe one day, even Stratford-upon-Avon.
DAVID LOCKE

► As the evening turns to dusk, GWR 'Hall' 4-6-0 No. 5972 *Olton Hall* takes water at Hellifield, North Yorkshire, whilst heading from its base at Carnforth to London King's Cross for filming of *Harry Potter and the Philosopher's Stone* on January 15 2001. It was painted in this bright red livery and renamed *Hogwarts Castle* for the filming.
EDDIE BOBROWSKI

◄ Sixty three years to the day after it was outshopped, brand new at the LMS' Crewe Works, 'Pacific' 4-6-2 No. 6233 *Duchess of Sutherland* has just arrived in Derby with an evening 'running-in' excursion – the appropriately titled 'Night Owl' – following its restoration. The 14-coach train on July 18 2001 was full with 600 people and took a circular route around the North Midlands.
PAUL ROBERTSON

▲ There's not a soul about at nightfall in Barrow Hill shed yard on July 12 2002. Left to its own devices, Midland Railway Johnson '1F' 0-6-0T No. 41708 of 1880 vintage, simmers gently under the yard lights alongside LMS Ivatt '2MT' 2-6-2T No. 41312.
JOHN BUNTING.

▶ Based on LNER 'Pacifics' the 15in gauge locomotives of the Romney, Hythe & Dymchurch Railway are just as impressive as their full-size cousins, despite being one-third their size. On September 10 2000 'Pacific' No. 8 *Hurricane* waits at Dungeness station with an evening train.
ANTHONY CROWHURST

▼ A shaft of low sunlight pierces through the wheels of LMS Fowler 'Crab' 2-6-0 No. 42765 at Burrs, East Lancashire Railway, on February 15 2003.
EDDIE BOBROWSKI

A Great Western Railway line-up in the style of publicity photographs from the 1930s. From the front are GWR 4-6-0 No. 6998 *Burton Agnes Hall*, 'Heavy Freight' 2-8-0 No. 3822, 'Castle' 4-6-0 No. 5051 *Earl Bathurst* and 'Hall' 4-6-0 No. 5900 *Hinderton Hall*.
MIKE McCORMAC

◀ In a cameo which could almost have been taken in the 1960s, Severn Valley Railway-based LMS '8F' 2-8-0 No. 48773 stands at Bury Bolton Street, East Lancashire Railway, on February 25 2002. The yellow stripe on the cabside was applied to locomotives to indicate that they were not allowed south of Crewe under the newly-electrified overhead wires in the 1960s. The star beneath the numbers shows that the locomotive's wheels are balanced for higher speed running.
BRIAN DOBBS

▶ Giants at rest. BR Standard '9F' 2-10-0 No. 92212 and LMS '8F' 2-8-0 No. 48773 glint in the yard at Buckley Wells, East Lancashire Railway, on January 25 2002.
L. STANFORD

▶ A face peeps through the booking office window at Quorn & Woodhouse station, Great Central Railway, but it's not that of a passing traveller. On January 16 2002 BR Standard '4MT' 4-6-0 No. 75014 pauses outside in the cold, whilst inside, you can almost hear the clock ticking as it marks the passing of time.
SIMON HOPKINS

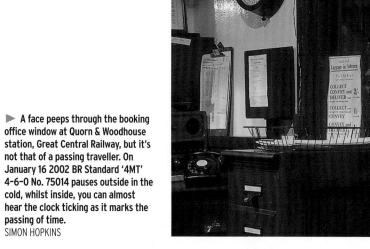

▲ A Great Western Railway signal stands clearly outlined against the sky as LMS 'Black Five' 4-6-0 No. 45110 stands at Bewdley station, Severn Valley Railway, on October 19 2001. Leaking steam and the warm glow of the fire from the cab, complete an atmospheric scene.
SIMON HOPKINS

▶ With night closing in around Holt, North Norfolk Railway, Worsdell 'J15' 0-6-0 No. 65462 waits patiently for the steam crane to lift out a 60ft length of rail. This was the first step towards installing a new point.
MICHAEL WILD

◀ Lit only by gas lamps, the stone-built station at Haworth, Keighley & Worth Valley Railway, has seen its last passengers for the evening, whilst BR Standard '4MT' 2-6-4T No. 80002 prepares for the 'right away'. The maroon embellishments indicate that this station is under London Midland Region control, which until 1954 it was. It then passed to the North Eastern Region, known for its tangerine signage and branding. The locomotive at this time would have been almost new, being built in 1952, as the third of a class totalling 155.
MALCOLM RANIERI

▲ Steam hisses and doors bang at Winchcombe station, Gloucestershire Warwickshire Railway, as LMS '2MT' 2-6-2T No. 41312 waits to depart for Toddington on May 12 2001. The station building, originally at Monmouth Troy, was removed stone-by-stone to Gloucestershire by the line's volunteers, who re-erected it at Winchcombe. The original station building here was demolished by BR before the line's closure in 1976.
MIKE TYACK